# There are lots more ideas where these came from.

This book is only one of an entire library of **Ideas** volumes that are available from Youth Specialties. Each volume is completely different and contains tons of tried and tested programming ideas submitted by the world's most creative youth workers. Order the others by using the form below.

## Combo Books

52 volumes of **Ideas** have been updated and republished in four-volume combinations. For example, our combo book **Ideas 1-4** is actually four books in one—volumes 1 through 4. These combos are a bargain at $19.95 each (that's 50% off!).

*SAVE UP TO 50%!*

## The Entire Library

The **Ideas** library includes every volume and an index to volumes 1-52. See the form below for the current price, or call the Youth Specialties Order Center at 800/776-8008.

---

# IDEAS ORDER FORM (or call 800/776-8008)

**COMBOS**
($19.95 each)
- ❏ Ideas 1-4
- ❏ Ideas 5-8
- ❏ Ideas 9-12
- ❏ Ideas 13-16
- ❏ Ideas 17-20
- ❏ Ideas 21-24
- ❏ Ideas 25-28
- ❏ Ideas 29-32
- ❏ Ideas 33-36
- ❏ Ideas 37-40
- ❏ Ideas 41-44
- ❏ Ideas 45-48
- ❏ Ideas 49-52

**SINGLES**
($9.95 each)
- ❏ Ideas 53
- ❏ Ideas 54
- ❏ Index to volumes 1-52

❏ **Entire Ideas Library**—54 volumes and Index (volumes 1-52) for only $199.95 (regularly $289-save over 30%!)

| SHIPPING CHARGES | |
|---|---|
| ORDER SUBTOTAL | ADD |
| $ 1.00- 9.99 | $3 |
| $ 10.00- 24.99 | $4 |
| $ 25.00- 49.99 | $6 |
| $ 50.00- 74.99 | $7 |
| $ 75.00- 99.99 | $9 |
| $ 100.00 AND UP | $10 |

PAYMENT METHOD:
- ❏ Check or money order enclosed. (CA residents add 7% sales tax; SC residents add 5% sales tax.)
- ❏ Credit card: ❏ Visa  ❏ MasterCard  Acct. # _____

Name on card: _____ Exp. _____
- ❏ Please bill me. (Shipping charges plus a 5% billing fee will be added to the total.)

NAME _____

CHURCH OR ORG. (IF APPLICABLE) _____

STREET ADDRESS _____

CITY _____ STATE _____ ZIP _____

DAYTIME PHONE (_____) _____

Clip and mail to Youth Specialties, P.O. Box 4406, Spartanburg, SC 29305-4406
or call 800/776-8008
Prices subject to change.

# Your Idea May Be Worth $100

It's worth at least $25 if we publish it in a future volume of **Ideas**. And it's worth $100 if it's chosen as the outstanding idea of the book it appears in.

It's not really a contest, though—just our way of saying thanks for sharing your creativity with us. If you have a good idea that worked well with your group, send it in. We'll look it over and decide whether or not we can include it in a future **Ideas** book. If we do, we'll send you at least 25 bucks!

In addition to that, the **Ideas** editor will select one especially creative idea from each new book as the outstanding idea of that particular book—and send a check for $100 to its contributor.

So don't let your good ideas go to waste. Write them down and send them to us, accompanied by this form. Explain your ideas completely (without getting ridiculous) and include illustrations, diagrams, photos, samples, or any other materials you think are helpful.

## FILL OUT BELOW

Name _____

Address_____

City _____ State ___ Zip _____

Phone (_____) _____

Write or type your idea(s) (one idea per sheet) and attach it to this form or to a copy of this form. Include your name and address with each idea you send. Mail to Ideas, 1224 Greenfield Drive, El Cajon, CA 92021. Ideas submitted to Youth Specialties cannot be returned.

# Ideas

## number fifty-three

Edited by
**Tim McLaughlin**

Illustrations by
**Robert Suggs**

ISBN 0-910125-38-4 (Ideas Single 53)
ISBN 0-910125-00-7 (Ideas Library)
© 1994 by Youth Specialties
1224 Greenfield Drive, El Cajon, CA 92021
619/440-2333

Ideas in this book have been voluntarily submitted by individuals and groups who claim to have used them in one form or another with their youth groups. Before you use an idea, evaluate it for its suitability to your own group, for any potential risks, for safety precautions that must be taken, and for advance preparation that may be required. Youth Specialties, Inc., is not responsible for, nor has it any control over, the use or misuse of any of the ideas published in this book.

# IDEAS • 53

# CONTENTS

# CHAPTER ONE

# GAMES

## Assault

Adapt the "Assault" game of TV's "American Gladiators" to your church hall or youth room. Set up the playing area with four barriers, such as tables and desks, for runners to hide behind. Set aside a small area for the "gladiators" to stay in, and designate a finish area. Provide 50 or more tennis balls for the gladiators to use. Supply safety gear—goggles, head gear, knee pads, etc.—for runners to use while running the course.

Give each runner one minute to run the course: from the start area to each of the barriers, trying to finish the course as quickly as possible—despite the barrage of tennis balls thrown by a pair of gladiators. Runners hit by a tennis ball are out.

Heighten the competition by placing an eight-foot-high target on the wall behind the gladiators. Then place a tennis ball behind each barrier. A runner successfully reaching a barrier may throw the tennis

ball there. Players who hit the target win the round.

Record the times of those who finish the course, and reward the fastest times with an American Gladiator T-shirt or similar prize. *Bruce Smith, Dinuba, Calif.*

## Back to School Shuffle

Form teams of eight students. Provide each team with a "locker" filled with items representing different classes in school: globe or map (history); calculator (math); gym clothes or tennis racket (P.E.); hammer (woodshop); paperback novel (English); protective goggles, beaker, or copy of the periodic table (chemistry); spatula or oven mitt (home economics); rubber nightcrawler (biology); sheet music (choir); brown bag or baloney sandwich in a Baggie (lunch); etc. Add other class subjects as desired.

Use page 8 to make a transparency (for an overhead projector), or you can write your own schedules on a flip chart. Reveal the schedules one at a time; as you uncover each schedule, team members must rush to their locker, retrieve the correct items, return to the starting point, and line up in the correct order. The first team to do so wins the round.

Team members lining up out of order are sent to detention and sit out a round. Offer each person on the winning team a small and/or silly prize—an apple, eraser, folder, etc. *Dennis Leggett, Seattle, Wash.*

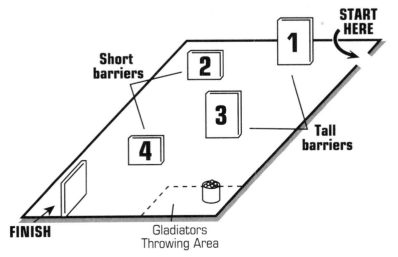

**START HERE**

**Short barriers**

**Tall barriers**

**FINISH**

Gladiators Throwing Area

## Beat Your Body

This teenage version of Duck Duck Goose is set up like this: a circle of chairs facing outward, one chair per

# BACK TO SCHOOL SHUFFLE

**PERIOD**

1 history
2 math
3 P.E.
4 woodshop

**LUNCHLUNCHLUNCH**

5 English
6 choir
7 Spanish

**PERIOD**

1 P.E.
2 English
3 home ec.
4 chemistry

**LUNCHLUNCHLUNCH**

5 math
6 history
7 band

**PERIOD**

1 woodshop
2 English
3 choir
4 Spanish

**LUNCHLUNCHLUNCH**

5 P.E.
6 biology
7 history

**PERIOD**

1 band
2 history
3 biology
4 chemistry

**LUNCHLUNCHLUNCH**

5 home ec.
6 English
7 P.E.

**PERIOD**

1 home ec.
2 English
3 P.E.
4 choir

**LUNCHLUNCHLUNCH**

5 Spanish
6 math
7 history

**PERIOD**

1 band
2 history
3 biology
4 P.E.

**LUNCHLUNCHLUNCH**

5 English
6 chemistry
7 woodshop

person in the youth group—except for the person designated "It."

In the center of the circle, place a garbage can (or a chair). "It" stands anywhere within the circle, holding a newspaper that is rolled and taped shut.

"It" walks around the inside of the circle, then taps someone on the shoulder with the newspaper—at which point "It" runs to the garbage can in the center of the circle, places the paper on the can (if the newspaper falls off, "It" must put the paper back on the can), and bolts for the chair of the individual she tapped.

The player who is tapped must run to the garbage can, grab the newspaper, and tap "It" before she reaches the vacated chair. If "It" reaches the chair and sits without being tapped, the new person becomes "It." If "It" gets tapped, that person remains "It" for another round.

Set a time limit, because this game can go forever. *Jon Pierce, Omaha, Neb.*

## Human Twisters

First number each player:
➤ **Up to six players:** Number them one through six. (The roll of the die will indicate which kid plays in a given turn.)

➤ **Seven to 11 players:** Number them 2 through 12. (The total of the roll of a pair of dice will indicate which player plays in a given turn.)

➤ **12 to 21 players:** Number them according to possible combinations of a pair of dice: 1:1, 1:2, 1:3, etc. (Sally, for instance, is 1:3; Bill is 2:5; Mark is 6:4.)

Next, number body parts. For example: the right ear is one, the left ear two, the right hand three, the left hand four, the right foot five, and the left foot six.

Your first roll is for the person; the second roll, for his or her body part. Say you're playing with 12 players or more. Your first roll is a 6:4 (that indicates which player—Mark, in this case) and your second roll is a 2 (that indicates Mark's left ear). The next pair of rolls is a 2:5 and a 3, which indicate Bill's right hand—so Mark places his left ear against Bill's right hand. The next thing you know, every person in the youth group is attached in one giant puzzle.

Whether you play this game competitively or just for laughs, it's still a lot of fun. This might be a good game to capture on film. Hang the less-embarrassing photos in the youth room. *Dik LaPine, Auburn Hills, Mich.*

## Blind Basketball

You'll need a Nerf basketball hoop, a ball, and two blindfolds.

Divide the group into two teams, one offense, the other defense. Blindfold one member of each team; these two will do the actual playing. Following the verbal instructions of their teammates, the blindfolded offensive player tries to find the hoop and make a basket; the blindfolded defensive player, doing his best to hear his team's instructions, defends the basket.

Play periods of five minutes or so, then offensive and defensive teams switch and new players are blindfolded. Also during the switch, move the hoop so the blindfolded players don't know where it is.

Reference the game later when you want to illustrate how we are bombarded by messages and need to be selective about whom we listen to. *Randy Isola, Chicago, Ill.*

## Centipede Wars

Make several "centipedes"—each centipede is five (or so) students, standing in a line, with their hands on the shoulders of the person in front of them.

The first person of each centipede is the "striker," who attempts to eliminate "segments" (individuals) in other centipedes by throwing a ball at a rival centipede's *rear* segment. (Balls must strike the players

below the neck.) When a centipede's hindmost segment is struck by a ball, that person drops out of the game. A centipede remains alive until the segment behind the striker is hit. Centipedes can maneuver anywhere in the playing area, but must remain attached at all times.

After a couple rounds, your teens will develop their own strategies for protecting the rear section while maneuvering to attack other centipedes. *Tom Lytle, Marion, Ohio*

# Chairball II

Junior highers love this one. A person sits on a revolving, rolling office chair in the center of a circle of players, who throw a ball at the *chair*. The sitter, meanwhile, attempts to block shots against his chair. Whoever hits the chair with the ball becomes the new sitter.

With a little practice, a sitter becomes pretty good at spinning, rolling, and twisting as he dodges the ball. The back of the chair, on the other hand, makes a great target for throwers. *Steve Smoker, Roanoke, Va.*

# Create a Game Night

So you can't find just the right game for your group? Let your kids create their own!

Empty your game closet of all the equipment: Hula-Hoops, basketballs, volleyballs, Frisbees, rope, tennis balls, hockey sticks—everything. Divide your group into teams of six to eight kids, and give them several pieces of game equipment. Their task: To invent a game using *all* their assigned equipment. When the creative juices begin flowing, the results are incredible.

After giving the teams time to devise their own games, call them all together to play each other's games. *Allen L. Pickett, Allison Park, Pa..*

# Food Transport Relays

Both these relay races involve carrying food from a near table, sitting next to each team line, to a far one—all without using one's hands. The results are delightfully messy.

## ➤ Flour Dripping

On each team's near table is a large bowl filled with flour. On the far table is a similar, though empty, bowl. Each player receives a six-ounce Styrofoam cup.

One at a time, holding the cup with teeth only (no hands allowed), a student fills the cup with flour. Then she runs across the room to the other table, and—still using no hands—dumps as much flour as possible into the empty bowl there. When all players have run once, the team that transferred the most flour wins.

## ➤ Puffed Rice Relay

On each near table is a bowl of water or milk and a bowl of puffed rice cereal. Far tables each have an empty bowl on them.

At "Go!" the first player in line dips his face into the water or milk, and then into the bowl of cereal (oatmeal works well, too). The goal is to get as much cereal stuck to his face as possible. As usual, no hands allowed.

Now the player with the puffed-rice face dashes to his team's far table, where he tries to get the cereal off his face and into the bowl—still without hands. When all players are done, the team with the most cereal in the bowl wins. *Bret Luallen, Cleveland, Okla.*

# Pick a Pic

Fill a basket or sack with pictures cut out of newspapers and magazines. Divide your group into at least two teams, each of which sends a person to the basket to pull out a picture. The teams then have 30 seconds to start a story, in writing, about the illustration.

After 30 seconds, teams send another person for another picture; each group *continues* the story, but somehow including the new picture. This continues until all teens have chosen pictures. Judges determine the team with the most creative story.

Paste the pictures on paper and intersperse them with pages from the stories. *Grant Medford, Springfield, Ill.*

# Four on a Couch

This is best played with at least 20 players. Write everyone's name on a slip of paper, one name per slip, and place them in a container.

Now sit everyone in a circle, with the couch (or four chairs) as part of the circle. Two boys and two girls (alternating) should sit on the couch. The teens sitting on the floor in a circle should leave one empty space.

Your goal: to fill the four spaces on the couch with either all boys or all girls.

Once your teens are all situated, have each player

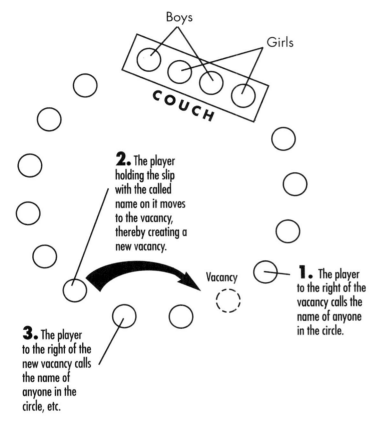

Boys
Girls
COUCH

**2.** The player holding the slip with the called name on it moves to the vacancy, thereby creating a new vacancy.

Vacancy

**1.** The player to the right of the vacancy calls the name of anyone in the circle.

**3.** The player to the right of the new vacancy calls the name of anyone in the circle, etc.

draw a name from the container. Then start with the person sitting to the right of the open space: he calls the name of anyone in the group. Whoever holds the slip of paper with that name on it moves to the open spot and trades slips with the person who called the name. The play continues: the person who sits to the right of the newly vacant spot now calls out a name. (Two turns must pass before the same name is called again.)

Clue: Pay attention, especially to the last name called. Other players may not give hints to the player whose turn it is. *Christopher Graham, Santa Barbara, Calif.*

# Frisbee Timer Tag

On a large, flat playing field with clearly marked boundaries, divide players into two teams. Each team's members decide how long they think they can

keep possession of the Frisbee.

Then teams gather near the center for the toss out: the referee-timer throws the Frisbee into any part of the field to begin the game. The clock begins when a player touches the Frisbee and continues until that player is tagged *or* the Frisbee touches the ground. Players may run with the Frisbee or throw it to another team member. The offensive team's captain yells out the estimated time and keeps up with points.

**Scoring.** A team receives points when it retains possession of the Frisbee for the amount of seconds the members estimated. Points received are equal to the number of seconds the team members estimated they could possess the Frisbee.

**Turnovers.** A team relinquishes possession of the Frisbee to their opponents when—

➤ The Frisbee touches the ground.
➤ The Frisbee or the player possessing it goes out-of-bounds.
➤ The player with the Frisbee is tagged by an opponent.
➤ The player with the Frisbee runs out-of-bounds to avoid being tagged.

After a period of play, let teams make new estimates of their possession time before resuming the game. *Greg Miller, Knoxville, Tenn.*

# Improv Games

Take advantage of stand-up comedy's popularity with an evening of improv comedy competition. Select teams and an emcee, and get ready for an

UM... ME? WELL, LET'S SEE, SO THEN THAT CHIPMUNK DUDE, THE 8-FOOT ONE, HE, LIKE, JUMPS INTO THE EVIL CLOWN'S HAIR, O.K? AND THE, UM, GREEN ARMADILLO, LIKE, FALLS THROUGH THIS TRAP DOOR?.. AND

DIE. DIE DIE DIE

I WAS ABOUT TO GET TO THE GOOD PART.

evening of laughter and memories. Here are some ideas to get things rolling.

### ➤ Lists.

Select two people from each team. Ask the audience for a list of 10 emotions or states of mind (rage, euphoria, panic, etc.). Write them down. Then ask the audience for an infrequent household chore, such as taking down the Christmas tree.

One of the teams begins acting out the chore, using words and actions, and conveying the first emotion on the list. Every 30 seconds or so, the emcee calls out a different one of the 10 emotions. The actors change emotions immediately, carrying out the same chore. Switch teams and repeat the process. Use the ol' "applause meter" to determine the winner.

### ➤ Talk or Die.

Select one person from each team and have those selected line up, facing the audience. The emcee begins a story, stopping halfway through a sentence and pointing to one of the players, who then continues the story. For example, the emcee says, "Two small children were standing in front of a candy store when, to their amazement—"

If a contestant hesitates or continues the story in a way that makes no sense, the audience and the emcee yell, "Die!" The last person standing is the winner.

### ➤ Video Fairy Tales.

Ask the audience to list types of movies—musicals, romantic comedies, police dramas, horror, sci-fi, techno-thrillers, spaghetti westerns, etc. Write them down, and each team picks one of the types. Then ask the audience for a popular fairy tale or nursery rhyme.

Give each team two minutes to plan how to enact the fairy tale or nursery rhyme in the cinematic genre they selected.

Appoint a "distinguished panel" of judges to score the acts on a scale of one to 10. Encourage the audience to voice approval or disapproval of the judges' decision.

*Kevin Turner, Tacoma, Wash.*

---

## Spitfire

Give each player a Styrofoam cup, a straw, and about 20 Q-Tips. Then pair off everyone.

Pairs sit facing each other with their Styrofoam cups on their heads. The aim of "Spitfire" is to shoot your partner's cup off his head by using the straw as a blowgun and the Q-Tips as ammunition.

You can score it any number of ways—for example, the one who shoots the cup off a partner's head the most times in one minute is the winner. Or play elimination-style until only one player is left. *Jim Ramos, Atascadero, Calif.*

---

## The Newly Taught Game

In the spirit of "The Newlywed Game," pair three or four Sunday school teachers with one pupil each from their classes. The teachers then leave the room. While they're gone, the emcee asks questions of the class members. The class members must answer the questions as they believe the teacher would answer them.

After returning to the room, the teacher is asked

the same questions. Each time the teacher's answer matches the pupil's, the pair gains points. For round two, send the pupils out of the room and have teachers answer questions as they believe their students will answer them.

Sample questions:

➤ Name the first person who arrives in your class most weeks.

➤ What was last week's lesson about?

➤ Which student in class adds the most to the discussion?

➤ What's been the funniest event in your class recently?

➤ Who's the newest member of your class?

➤ Who would be a good prospective member for your class?

➤ Who does your teacher resemble most when teaching—the Terminator, Elizabeth II, Fred Flintstone, Bette Midler, Clark Kent, or Mary Lou Retton?

➤ What will your teacher say your class resembles most: a well-drilled team, a barrel of monkeys, a team of scientists.

Get as creative as you can with your questions. You can also broaden this game to pair up any youth worker with any student. *John Peters, Cleveland, Tenn.*

# Over and Back

All you need for this high-action game is dice (just one die, actually), a whistle, a watch, two scorekeepers, a timekeeper, and a room divided by a masking-tape line on the floor.

Split your students into two teams, placing the teams on opposite sides of the room. One team is the Odd Team; the other, the Even Team. The timekeeper stands on the sideline and begins play by rolling a die. Depending on the roll, he then calls out "Odd!" or "Even!" The team whose name he calls immediately crosses into enemy territory and tries to pull other team members across the line. They get a point for every opposing player they can pull across.

Meanwhile, the die is rolled every five seconds. If the roll changes from odd to even, the whistle is blown and the task of the players changes. Those who are in enemy territory must exit without getting tagged; otherwise, the other team gets a point.

At the end of one minute, the round ends with three short whistle blasts. The scorekeeper

announces the scores for the round. Play resumes with a 0-0 score for each round. Winners are announced as the best of five rounds. *Frank Riley, Simi Valley, Calif.*

# Pew Soccer

Divide your students into one team per section of pews in your auditorium. One player from each team goes to the front of the auditorium; the rest find places under the pews in their section.

Here's what kids do under the pews: starting at the front of the church, they move an inflated balloon to the back of the auditorium. If the balloon escapes through the sides, the person at the front must retrieve it and start the whole process again for his section. You can make the game more interesting by restricting *how* the students move the balloon—prohibit the use of hands, the use of legs, etc. *Len Cuthbert, Hamilton, Ont., Canada*

# Ninja

For this game you need 10 soft foam rings (or five-inch circles cut from cardboard), a piano bench (or step stool), and masking tape to mark the "danger zone"—a strip running the full width across the cen-

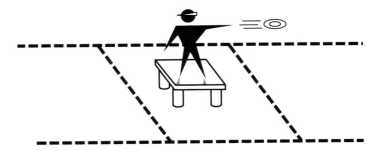

ter of the room.

Select one person to be The Ninja. Give him the rings and stand him on the piano bench, where he must stay during play.

Line up the rest of your group at one end of the room. On "Go!" they try to run past The Ninja without being "killed" (hit by a ring); because runners may not feel the rings hitting them, officials determine who is hit. Players who are killed must remain in the danger zone for the rest of the game.

Once they are confined to the danger zone, how-

ever, dead players can try to slow down live players from leaving the danger zone, but without holding onto them. "Dead" players can also retrieve rings for The Ninja. "Live" runners keep passing back and forth through the danger zone until only one is left: the next Ninja. *Doug Partin, Artesia, N.Mex.*

# Psycho

Prime your group for this game by showing Alfred Hitchcock's classic *Psycho* at your next lock-in. Also in advance of the game, select five students—one to play the psycho, four to play detectives. Keep their identities secret from each other and from the group at large. Only you know their identities, and they are to tell no one who they are.

After the movie announce that a psycho is in your midst—the individual looks perfectly normal and could be anyone. Fortunately, there are four undercover detectives on the job to catch the psycho—but they must catch him *in the act*.

The psycho must wear a wig at the time of attack and must mark the victims with a felt-tip marker. (Hide the wig and marker prior to the game and let the psycho know where to retrieve them when the game begins.) Provide pocket New Testaments to your four detectives as badges and proof of their identities. The detectives can make an arrest only if they catch the psycho in the act, wig and all.

Release everyone to go and hide from the psycho throughout the darkened building. But warn them to be careful—the psycho might be hiding with them! Once the psycho marks a victim, that person must return to the youth room to await the outcome of the game.

This game ends one of two ways: either a detective catches the psycho in the act, or the psycho attacks and gets rid of all the detectives before any of the four can apprehend the psycho. *Jason McClelland and David Moss, Tampa, Fla.*

# Rubber Band Dance

Divide players into at least two teams. Line them up, relay fashion. Give each team a giant rubber band (or three or four XXL ones from your office supply). When the whistle blows, each team's first player pulls the rubber band over his entire body, passing it on to the teammate behind him. The first team done wins.

Plan to have a camcorder ready: videotape the kids as they're gyrating, trying to get the rubber band over their heads and down around their waists. Play the videotape back to Glenn Miller's "In the Mood," and viewers will swear that the kids are doing some crazy, strange dance. *Jim Mitchell, Fairbanks, Alaska*

# CHAPTER TWO

# CREATIVE COMMUNICATION

## Cookie Bake

Illustrate how believers need each other while creating the evening's snack—make chocolate chip cookies.

Write on poster board a recipe for mouth-watering chocolate chip cookies, and hang it outside the church kitchen door. Gather all the ingredients needed to make the cookies, as well as the utensils you need— bowl, mixing spoon, cookie sheets, pot holders, metal spatulas. Divide participants into groups of four, and assign one person in each group one of the following roles.

➤ **Messenger** is the only one who can look at the recipe. Messenger can neither speak nor walk, however. Messenger writes out each step at the proper time, and Guide carries Messenger to deliver the writing to Encourager.

➤ **Arms** is the blindfolded player who mixes ingredients together.

➤ **Guide** carries Messenger to deliver the recipe, but Guide's mouth is taped shut.

➤ **Encourager**, seated in a chair through the whole process, receives written recipe steps from Messenger and tells Arms what to do to make the cookies. Encourager inspires all the team's participants to work fast and efficiently.

After each team mixes up a batch of dough, everyone forms and bakes the cookies. While the cookies are baking, read and discuss 1 Corinthians 12:12-31 (spiritual gifts given for the common good). Conclude by eating the cookies fresh from the oven.
*Glenn Balzer, Littleton, Colo.*

## Describe the Counselor

Illustrate the accuracy of the gospels' description of Jesus, using your teens' own powers of observation. This works best with at least five groups with three members each.

Pick a well-known adult volunteer or youth leader (someone with a healthy self-image) who is absent from your meeting. Divide into groups, assigning someone who can draw to each group.

Ask the group members to come up with seven things about "Bill" that characterize him. The first four things can be nonphysical descriptions (he's our youth pastor, he's married to Andrea, he drives a red Mustang, he lives in Utica). The next three things should describe his character or specific events about him that stick out as memorable (he does impressions, he always runs late, he built an igloo at the retreat). The group members must agree on each of the descriptions. The goal is to match as many descriptions as possible with the other groups.

Next, have each group's artist draw a picture of Bill from memory only.

Bring the groups together to compare descriptions and pictures. Find the things all the groups had in common (usually there are two or three things all groups agree on). Make the point to your students that many people who know one person can come up with a pretty accurate description of that person. The gospel writers had some basic common descriptions of Jesus and the things he did, so the post-resurrection appearances of Christ could not have been hallucinations. *Bill Fry, New Hartford, N.Y.*

# Driving Lesson

Communicating the lordship of Christ to high school freshmen and sophomores by giving them a chance behind your car's wheel really gets the point across. You will, of course, need to get parents' permission before this event.

While the youths are participating in some social activity inside the church, one by one take the freshmen and sophomores outside. Give each student the keys to your car, which is parked just outside the door.

Explain the activity to each student: "I want you to drive my car around the parking lot for a few minutes, going no faster than 25 m.p.h. Once you and I are inside the car, however, I am officially ignorant of how to operate and drive it, so asking for my advice won't help. The only time I will interfere is if you are about to hit something or you lose control."

(It's a riot watching these younger high schoolers—most of whom have never driven before—try to find the ignition, the lights, figure out how to engage the transmission, etc.)

Halfway around the parking lot, explain that you aren't doing this because you want to be the coolest youth pastor of all time (though, of course, you are). Tell them something like this:

*I'm a better driver than you are, and I like being in control. It's difficult for me to let an inexperienced and nervous person like you drive. Likewise, God is better at directing your life than you are, and he would rather you gave him control since you are inexperienced and unsure of life's road. That's the real sign of letting Christ be Lord of your life—when you let him be in control.*

After each student parks as close as possible to the original parking spot (a laugh in itself), pray with the student and hand him or her a 3 x 5 note card with a key glued to it. The card lists verses about the importance of giving God control each day. Ask each student to keep secret from the rest of the group what happened outside.

This activity can be a success (but not a smashing one, we hope) and can stimulate great group discussions after you've done this with several students. *Kevin Conklin, Deerfield, Ill.*

# Family Choices

Use this game (reminiscent of the board game Life) to launch your lessons about family life—family choices, dynamics, and communication skills. Your kids will get to know each other a little better, and may even learn some negotiation skills that will benefit their own family life.

Divide your students into "families" of four, preferably two boys and two girls; at the least, one girl in a family of boys or one boy in a family of girls. Use an arbitrary way to select two parents for each group—choosing a number between one and four, etc. A group's only male or only female is automatically one of the parents.

Supply each family with the materials to make simple, throw-away spinners (see page 18 for instructions), or make enough spinners yourself beforehand. Then pass out copies of the "Family Choices" worksheet (page 17) for families to fill in. When everyone's finished, ask each family to share its answers with the group.

Finally, take Polaroids of each family and display them in your youth room. *Rob Marin, Whittier, Calif.*

# FAMILY CHOICES

1. Rename the cereal Froot Loops.

2. Figure out a last name for your family.

3. Write down the country or state you want to live in.

4. Write down the kind and number of pets you have.

5. Write down your favorite homecooked meal and fast-food place.

6. Choose your favorite amusement park.

7. If your family were a planet, which planet would you be?

## Now use your spinner to determine—

8. Number of children your family will ultimately have: _____

9. The make of car you'll drive: _____

10. What you'll live in: _____

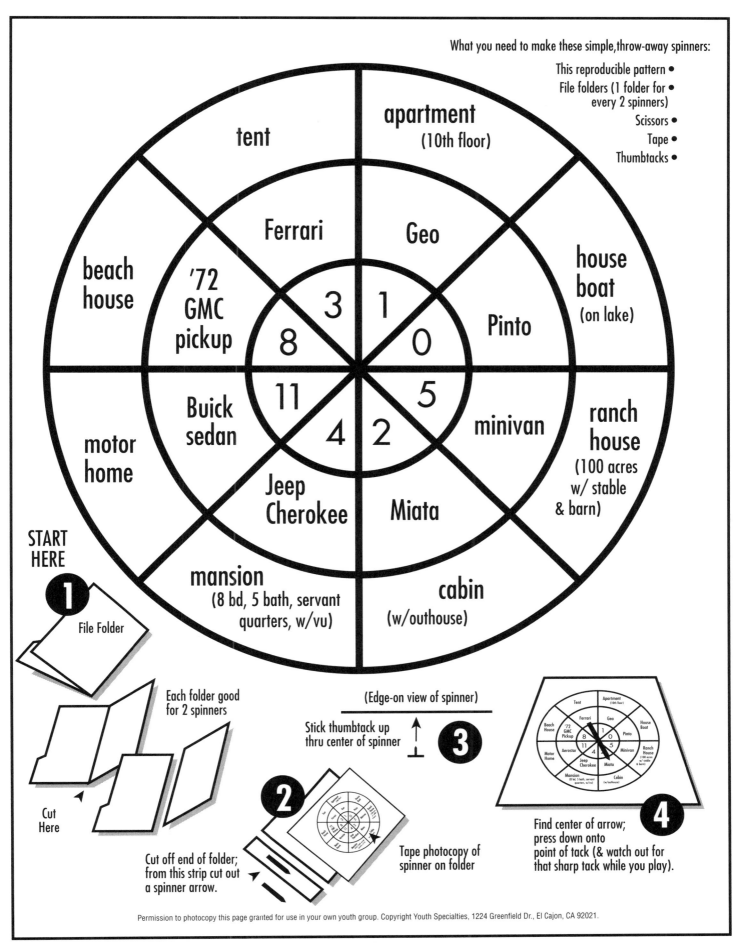

What you need to make these simple, throw-away spinners:

- This reproducible pattern •
- File folders (1 folder for •
  every 2 spinners)
- Scissors •
- Tape •
- Thumbtacks •

tent

apartment
(10th floor)

beach
house

Ferrari

Geo

house
boat
(on lake)

'72
GMC
pickup

3   1

Pinto

8   0

11   5

4   2

minivan

ranch
house
(100 acres
w/ stable
& barn)

Buick
sedan

motor
home

Jeep
Cherokee

Miata

cabin
(w/outhouse)

mansion
(8 bd, 5 bath, servant
quarters, w/vu)

START
HERE

**1**

File Folder

Each folder good
for 2 spinners

Cut
Here

(Edge-on view of spinner)

Stick thumbtack up
thru center of spinner

**3**

**2**

Cut off end of folder;
from this strip cut out
a spinner arrow.

Tape photocopy of
spinner on folder

Find center of arrow;
press down onto
point of tack (& watch out for
that sharp tack while you play).

**4**

# Jar of Favorites

In a fast-paced, always-changing world, here's an activity that can demonstrate the stability Christ gives. At a New Year's Eve party or other annual event, students fill out a sheet of favorite television shows, music groups and songs, foods, fashions, phrases—together with their favorite things about Jesus and the Bible. Collect these lists, put them in a jar, and bury it. A year later dig the jar up and see how much has changed—and what has remained the same. *John Peters, Cleveland, Tenn.*

---

# The Real Thing

Help young people tell the real thing from a look-alike by providing samples of several brands of cola drinks and letting your kids try to figure out which is Coca-Cola. Let them also try maple syrup and several brands that claim to taste just like it. Finally, have them compare regular milk to two percent, skim, and evaporated milk.

After completing several tastings, lead a discussion about what makes things phoney or real. Ask your group to list some things they perceive as phoney. Then ask them to list some things that they view as real.

Finally, discuss the reality of God. He really is (Rom. 1:18-20), he does what he says (Ps. 119:160), he loves us (John 3:16, Rom. 5:8), and he has a plan for us (Jer. 29:11, Prov. 3:5-6). *Mike McKay, Los Gatos, Calif.*

---

# Time Game

A hands-on object lesson in evaluating priorities, this game asks kids to literally fit their activities into specified periods of time in a diagram. Following the exercise, discuss making choices about how to spend time.

Hand out copies of the sheet (page 20, or design your own) and direct students to cut out the paper strips of activities. (However you adapt the list of "Activities"—for example, adding "finals" or "Christmas shopping" to reflect seasonal activities—make sure there are more activities than there is room on the "Your Day" box on page 21. Just like real life.) Then they place whichever strips they want—and can fit—into "Your Day" rectangle (page 21). Activity strips may not overlap.

When the students finish, ask questions like these to kick off discussion and reflection:

➤ *Do your choices reflect how you actually spend your time?*
➤ *Which activities did you leave out?*
➤ *How did you choose which ones to eliminate?*
➤ *How do you feel about the activities you left out?*
➤ *Why did you include certain activities?*
➤ *Did you choose activities out of obligation or genuine desire to include them?*
➤ *Do your choices of activities have anything to do with your long-term goals?*
➤ *How does your relationship with God affect which activities you included?*
➤ *Is Jesus' example of spending time helpful? (Mark 1:35-39 is one example of how Jesus managed his time.)*
➤ *How, if at all, has this discussion caused you to rethink your choices?*

*Tim Gerarden, Dubuque, Ia.*

---

# The Problem with Friends

Coach one of your theatrical students to give the monologue on page 22 as an introduction to a meeting about friendship—or give it yourself in teenage "costume." *Kyle White, Sycamore, Ill.*

---

# Students' Bill of Rights

Your students will be surprised what they *can* do as Christians on their school campuses when you distribute this bill of rights (see page 23). *Tom Lytle, Marion, Ohio*

---

# Theological Zoo Guide

Sometimes we take kids on excursions that are fun, but end up wishing that we could have done or experienced something with a little more substance. Try handing out the questions on page 24 as a devotional zoo guide the next time you take a trip to the zoo. *Pierre Allegre, Seattle, Wash.*

---

# Time Game

## Activities

washing dishes

brushing teeth

housework

church

prayer

homework

hanging out
with friends

talking on
the phone

TV

school

part-time job

school club
or sports

dating

movies

Nintendo

# Time Game

## Your Day

(Cut apart the Activities slips on the other sheet, then choose the ones you want to fill your day—this box. No overlapping!)

# THE PROBLEM WITH FRIENDS
## A Monologue

**H**ey. My name's Joel. I'd say I'm a pretty good friend—but not with just anybody. In fact, I have very few friends...(*on second thought, defensively*) but it's not because I'm a jerk.

I'm just picky.

Now take Bill. I've known Bill since we were in third grade. We used to do everything together. Once we had a bottle-rocket fight in my garage, and my parents never found out. Well, one time Bill was supposed to meet me at the mall, and we were supposed to hang out for the day and then his mom was supposed to give us a ride home. Well, Bill never shows, and I get stuck at the mall and my parents are all mad because they have to come pick me up. Bill said he forgot, but I said, "Forgot? Friends don't treat each other like that. You're a jerk, Bill."

I never spoke to him again.

Then there was Eric. We were pretty good friends, and we hung around with the same crowd at school. One day Eric told me his dad lost his job and they were on food stamps now. It was okay for a while, but pretty soon Eric couldn't afford to go to the movies with us, and his clothes started to look pretty dorky. His family moved out of their house—probably because they couldn't make payments on it anymore. I think they moved into low-income housing. I don't really talk to him anymore, but I see him in the hall once in a while at school.

Now Terri and I were good friends...for a while. The problem was, she started calling me every day. I just didn't have that kind of time to spend on the phone. She got mad because I didn't call her back for four days in a row. We don't hang out together anymore.

And Karen was pretty cool—until she started having all these problems at home. Then she started to ask if she could "talk" to me. What she <u>really</u> wanted was to dump all her problems on me. I thought, "No way!" but what I told her was, (*with a façade of kindness*) "Why don't you get back to me after you get your life together?" I mean, the last thing I need is someone who's just gonna bring me down.

Anyway...like I said, I'm pretty picky about my friends...(*an awkward pause*) Actually, I guess I don't have friends... (*stubbornly confident again*) I figure that friendship is a big gift I don't want to give to just any-one who comes along. I mean, you know how it is?

# *End*

# STUDENTS' BILL OF RIGHTS ON A PUBLIC SCHOOL CAMPUS

**I.** THE RIGHT TO MEET WITH OTHER RELIGIOUS STUDENTS.
The Equal Access Act allows students the freedom to meet on campus for the purpose of discussing religious issues.

**II.** THE RIGHT TO IDENTIFY YOUR RELIGIOUS BELIEFS THROUGH SIGNS AND SYMBOLS.
Students are free to express their religious beliefs through signs and symbols.

**III.** THE RIGHT TO TALK ABOUT YOUR RELIGIOUS BELIEFS ON CAMPUS.
Freedom of speech is a fundamental right mandated in the Constitution and is not nullified in the school yard.

**IV.** THE RIGHT TO DISTRIBUTE RELIGIOUS LITERATURE ON CAMPUS.
Distributing literature on campus may not be restricted simply because the literature is religious.

**V.** THE RIGHT TO PRAY ON CAMPUS.
Students may pray alone or with others so long as it does not disrupt school activities or is not forced on others.

**VI.** THE RIGHT TO CARRY OR STUDY YOUR BIBLE ON CAMPUS.
The Supreme Court has said that only *state directed* Bible reading is unconstitutional.

**VII.** THE RIGHT TO DO RESEARCH PAPERS, SPEECHES, AND CREATIVE PROJECTS WITH RELIGIOUS THEMES.
The First Amendment does not forbid all mention of religion in public schools.

**VIII.** THE RIGHT TO BE EXEMPT.
Students may be exempt from activities and class contents that contradict their religious beliefs.

**IX.** THE RIGHT TO CELEBRATE OR STUDY RELIGIOUS HOLIDAYS ON CAMPUS.
Music, art, literature, and drama that have religious themes are permitted as part of the curriculum for school activities if presented in an objective manner as a traditional part of the cultural and religious heritage of the particular holiday.

**X.** THE RIGHT TO MEET WITH SCHOOL OFFICIALS.
The First Amendment to the Constitution forbids Congress to make any law that would restrict the right of the people to petition the Government (school officials).

Reprinted with permission. The complete book *Students' Legal Rights* is available by writing or calling Roever Communications, P.O. Box 136130, Ft. Worth, TX 76136, phone 800/873-2839.

# Theological Zoo Guide

🐄 **Primates.** Watch them monkey around. Does "monkeying around" describe your walk with God? What do you need to do to get serious about God in your life? (1 Cor. 9:24-27)

🐄 **Giraffes.** Check out their necks, which help them to reach their food high in the trees. In your walk with God, are you stretching to reach spiritual food in the Bible, or are you only feeding off the crumbs on the floor? What are some things you can do to improve the reach of your devotional life? (Psa. 42:1-2)

🐄 **Hippos.** Two words best describe these "water horses": lazy and fat! That's okay if you're a hippo, but Christians can't afford to get spiritually lazy and fat by failing to apply God's Word to our lives. How have you applied the Word to your life this week? (Prov. 13:4; Heb. 6:11-12; James 2:14-20)

🐄 **Elephants.** These behemoths are a picture of strength and stability. As you consider your spiritual life, how strong and stable are you? What needs to happen in order for you to become a picture of spiritual strength and stability? (Eph. 6:10; 1 Cor. 15:58)

🐄 **Raptors.** Although you probably won't see the bald eagle there in flight, you can imagine what a majestic sight that would be, wings outstretched and soaring freely. Do you feel strong and free in your walk with God, or do you feel like the eagle in the zoo, chained to a post and just sitting there? What is keeping you from soaring strong and free like an eagle in the wild? (Isa. 40:31)

🐄 **Owls.** Notice the different species. We traditionally think of owls as being wise. Are you listening to wisdom in your life, or do you live foolishly? What advice have you been ignoring that you should pay attention to? (Prov. 2)

🐄 **Turkey vultures.** They're valuable to the environment because they feed on dead and rotting carcasses. (Is it lunch time yet?) We can feed our minds rotten garbage if we're not careful about the things we watch or listen to. How pure is your mind? What changes do you need to make in what you allow to enter your mind? (Phil. 4:8; Psa. 101:3)

🐄 **Gorillas.** Good communication within a tightly knit social group is important for their survival in dense forest. Just like the gorilla, we need each other to survive in our jungle. How tightly are you knitted to the youth group at church? Are you committed to building love and unity in our group? What are some things you can do in order to make it a place where everyone feels loved and accepted and is encouraged to love others? (Heb. 10:23-25)

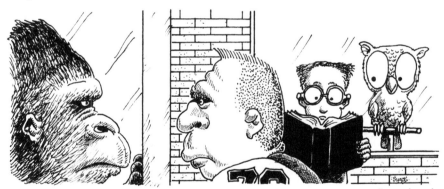

🐄 **Mountain goats.** These are known for their sure, nimble footing in rocky, dangerous terrain. Spiritually speaking, how sure and nimble is your footing? Are there things in your life that are causing you to stumble? What can you do to remove or get around those obstacles? (Matt. 18:7-9)

🐄 **Lions.** How alert would you be if you were dropped in the middle of that cage? The Bible says that Satan is like a roaring lion, seeking to devour us. What are you doing to resist his attacks? (1 Pet. 5:8-9)

🐄 **Reticulated python.** Check out his size! Satan's first appearance in the Bible is as a serpent in the Garden of Eden, where he deceived Eve into eating forbidden fruit. Have you been tempted to believe a lie that Satan has thrown at you in order to deceive you? How can you guard yourself against his deceit and trickery? (Gen. 3:1-6, 13)

Can you think of any other spiritual analogies related to any of the animals you saw today? Write down on the back as many as you can think of.

# Underground Church

To the catacombs! This is part adventure game, part worship and celebration. Your kids' first task in this evening event is to elude the Secret Police of a corrupt, anti-Christian government and locate Safe Houses run by the Christian underground. Then they travel to the Meeting House—a secret, secluded location for celebration and worship, with reminders of what ancient and modern Christians have endured in order to meet and worship together.

Get lots of people from church or the community involved—the evening requires planners, Contacts, Safe House owners, Secret Police, and worship-service organizers. (Delegate!) For practical safety reasons this game must be carried out in a carefully designated area, defined clearly on a map carried by all participants. Choose a neighborhood where traffic is minimal.

The details in the adventure game as explained below can be changed to suit your own community and group. Use more or fewer clues, arm the Secret Police with weapons other than Supersoakers, etc. Make it your event.

## BACKGROUND

The adventure setting is a police state where all Christian gatherings are outlawed. The religious underground has begun a resistance movement, however, to protect and encourage believers. They have organized a clandestine meeting of Christians in their neighborhood.

Thanks to old church membership lists, all believers have been organized into cell groups. For their own protection, they know the identities of neither their own cell members nor those in other cells.

On the event night they will locate their own cell's Safe House and be introduced to other cell members. Before the evening is over, they will meet with the other cells for worship and mutual encouragement.

A week before the event, underground leaders circulate special I.D. cards and bracelets to identify all believers (see "Publicity" below). I.D. cards are color coded, by cell group, with a small colored dot. Included with them is a map with the first of four clues that eventually lead to the Safe House for a particular cell group.

## THE TASK OF UNDERGROUND MEMBERS

On the night of the event—armed with color-coded I.D., bracelet, instruction sheet (page 27), map (an example is on page 26), and the first clue—kids get their next three clues from three Contacts: two Street Persons and a Store Owner/Manager/Clerk (see Instructions for Underground Contacts on page 28). Participants must move about in groups of three or four; groups fewer or larger than that are strictly forbidden.

When players approach someone they suspect is a Contact, they say the underground passwords: "Do you have any old newspapers to donate?" True Contacts respond, "Come walk on the water." Contacts then check kids' I.D.s, for they can give clues only to students with their color.

The fourth and final clue takes underground members to their Safe House, where they'll be blindfolded and driven to the secret gathering at the Meeting House.

Believers need a total of four dots on their I.D. card to get into the Safe House. The bracelet identifies participants to Contacts and other believers. No one is allowed into a Safe House without a bracelet.

As they're searching for Contacts and clues, they must also elude the Secret Police, who are intent on breaking up the resistence movement and discovering the members of the underground. They are everywhere that night, and they have no identifying signs—except that they are armed with Supersoakers. When the Secret Police catch believers, they remove their bracelets, blindfold them, and take them to prison.

## PRISON

"Prison" is a darkened room at the church. While sitting in the darkened room, prisoners hear sounds of interrogation, torture, and guns firing blanks. (Use good judgment as to how much realism is appropriate for your group.) From time to time the Secret Police remove one of the prisoners from the room; these are taken to another darkened room, but the people in the first room don't know where their comrades are.

In the end, underground commandos rescue their captured fellow believers and take them to the Meeting House, but the commandos act as if not everyone got out alive. Those who "died" can be memorialized at the worship service. Some groups make it so that the fatal circumstances of these "martyrs" resemble those of actual martyrs killed by repressive governments in our own day.

## THE CLANDESTINE CELEBRATION

At each of the Safe Houses, students are blindfolded and transported by vans and buses to the secret Meeting House—a nearby church, chapel, camp, or retreat center.

Conduct the celebration service according to your group's tastes. A typical one consists of—
➤ Upbeat, contemporary songs, as well as some somber, meditative songs.
➤ The narration or reading of actual persecution around the world, both ancient (check out "Catacomb Christians" in *Ideas 42*) and modern, intertwined with a couple fictitious stories about underground members who were lost that evening trying to get to this meeting.
➤ A challenging message.
➤ Concrete take-home symbols—salvation bracelets, I.D. cards, etc.—reminders of the underground experience.

After the celebration students are transported back to the starting point to be taken home.

## PUBLICITY

Here's how you can make this evening a big event—and even get some press coverage if you're lucky.

### Three weeks before the event
➤ Youth group members each receive a flier that invites them to a secret underground gathering—with a warning to watch out for the Secret Police. (Photocopy page 29 or design your own.)

### Two weeks before the event
➤ Polaroid photos of captured underground leaders—along with cassette tapes of their coerced confessions—are circulated at school.
➤ Run free radio spots on local stations, inviting kids to "Go Underground!" Spots include the date, time, and starting location.
➤ Students receive a Secret Police flier with the photo of a captured underground leader (see page 30; if you can, tape a photo of one of your kids over the existing photo). The message is clear: *Don't* go underground.

### One week before the event
➤ Students circulate underground bracelets and I.D. cards.
➤ Run a notice in your local paper warning residents that students will be participating in this adventure game.
➤ The Secret Police make home visits, warning kids not to go underground.
➤ Place signs strategically in neighborhood yards, reading "Go Underground!" and "Don't Go Underground!" or "Go Underground at Your Own Risk!"

*Skip Seibel, Greenville, Pa.*

# UNDERGROUND CHURCH
## INSTRUCTIONS FOR MEMBERS

We are now living in a police state. Christian gatherings are outlawed. Yet the underground has planned a clandestine meeting of area Christians and has circulated bracelets to identify all members.

### UNDERGROUND BRACELET

You must locate the Safe House with your bracelet intact. From your Safe House you will be transported to the secret gathering at the Meeting House.

### I.D. CARD AND COLOR-CODED ROUTES

You will be given an I.D. card with a colored circle and a street location. The street location will take you to your first contact, who will place a matching colored dot on your I.D. card—and give you another clue. From there you will continue your journey.

You must find a total of three Contacts, for a total of four colored dots on your I.D. card, before you will be able to enter your cell's own Safe House. There are many Safe Houses, but only one that will accept your color-coded I.D. card. Contacts can give clues only to underground church members whose cell color matches the dots they are carrying.

### PASSWORDS

To identify Contacts ask, "Do you have any old newspapers to donate?" Contacts will respond, "Come walk on the water." They will then determine if your color-coded I.D. card matches the color they can give out. Not all Contacts can give you your color dot.

### SECRET POLICE

On your way to the Safe House, you must elude the Secret Police. Beware! They are everywhere, and they are deadly! The Secret Police are armed with Supersoakers. If they "kill" you—that is, drench you—they will remove your bracelet and take you to prison. Once you are hit by water from a Supersoaker, there is no escape. Safe Houses will not admit anyone who is wet, even if the person has a bracelet and I.D. card.

### GROUP SIZE

You must move about in groups of three or four. Groups smaller than three and larger than four are strictly forbidden.

### CAN'T FIND THE SAFE HOUSE?

You have until 7 p.m. to find your Safe House. If you don't find your Safe House by 7 p.m., return to the starting point immediately. We will transport you from there to the underground Meeting House.

# INSTRUCTIONS FOR UNDERGROUND CONTACTS

**Date of event:** _____

**Time of event:** _____

**Name of Contact:** _____

Thanks for helping with Underground Church. We have _____ separate routes. Each one is color coded. Kids will come to you with an I.D. card, on the back of which is a colored dot. Give clues or directions *only* to kids with your color.

The game part of the evening will begins at _____ p.m. and concludes at _____ p.m.

### FIRST CONTACT: STREET PERSON 1

You can be anywhere on your assigned section of the street, doing whatever you like—loitering, reading, dumpster diving, talking with someone, talking to yourself, etc.

Underground members will ask you, "Do you have any old newspapers to donate?" Your response is, "Come walk on the water."

Check their I.D. card for your color dot. If the color is correct, place one of your dots on the I.D. card and give them the next clue. If they have a *different* color dot, give them neither one of your dots nor the next clue. (They must have four dots of the same color to be admitted to the Meeting House.)

### SECOND CONTACT: STORE OWNER/MANAGER/CLERK

Whether an office, restaurant, or retail store—greet kids in a businesslike manner ("How can I help you tonight?" or "Table for how many?" etc.). When they ask, "Do you have any old newspapers to donate?" quietly respond with "Come walk on the water."

Check all I.D.s for your color, then follow the same procedure as above.

### THIRD CONTACT: STREET PERSON 2

Your situation is similar to that of Street Person 1 (above); only be involved in something different. If Street Person 1 looks like a transient, for example, you may want to appear solidly middle-class, perhaps waiting for a bus or window shopping.

Follow the pattern explained above when kids approach you.

### FOURTH CONTACT: SAFE HOUSE

To make it fun, you can respond in one of several ways. Here are just a couple:

• Be suspicious and wary; don't immediately open the door when you hear the knock, but first peer through a window (but so the kids can see you) and perhaps even answer without opening the door, "Who is it?" or "What do you want?"

When the kids ask, "Do you have any old newspapers to donate?" *then* open the door and respond quietly with "Come walk on the water."

• Answer the door nonchalantly, as if you just stepped away from an animated—and State-approved—after-dinner conversation. When underground members ask you, "Do you have any old newspapers to donate?" answer in a way that throws them momentarily off guard: "Oh, I'm sorry, we don't keep newspapers—but if you want, you can come walk on the water."

However you respond, admit only those underground members who are not wet (those who've avoided the Secret Police's Supersoakers), who have the correct number and color of circles on their I.D. card, and who are still wearing their bracelet.

In the Safe House kids are blindfolded, then driven by van or bus to the Meeting House.

Come
walk
on the
water!

*Go*

# Underground

Date:_____

Place:_____

Time:_____

## Beware of the Secret Police!

# A WARNING FROM THE
# SECRET POLICE

Captured Underground Leader
This could be you!

# DON'T GO UNDERGROUND!

Date: _____

Place: _____

Time: _____

## A MESSAGE FROM YOUR LOCAL FRIENDLY SECRET POLICE

# *Writing a Personal Testimony*

Want to ensure that your discipleship group understands the importance of having a prepared testimony as they witness to their friends, or during mission or service trips?

This is part Bible study (page 32), part written exercise (page 33). If you can, photocopy the two pages onto opposite sides of the same sheet; otherwise, two sheets will work.

The Bible study on Paul's conversion is a good opener for your session. Use it inductively as the students read through Acts 26:1-23.

Then it's time for your kids to turn over the sheets and write their own testimonies. Talk through the sections of the worksheet, allowing kids to verbalize their individual responses to the questions before writing them down. After everyone finishes, ask some (or all) to share their testimonies with each other in small groups. *Vaughn Van Skiver, Bath, N.Y.*

# Writing Your Personal Testimony
## The Example of the Apostle Paul

One of the privileges and responsibilities of Christians is to share with others our faith in Christ. Although many methods and plans can be used to communicate our faith, none is more effective than sharing how the love, grace, and mercy of Christ has changed our lives.

People to whom we witness may evade issues, attempt to discredit biblical and historical facts, or blame their condition on others. But it's hard to discount the authentic testimony of a believer whose life has been transformed.

That's the reason for this lesson. Completing the worksheet will better equip you to give a logical and organized presentation of who Jesus Christ is and what he has done in your life.

Let's use the story of Paul's conversion as a pattern for your testimony.

*Read the Bible text: Acts 26:1-23*

## PAUL'S ATTITUDES AND ACTIONS BEFORE HIS CONVERSION—VV. 1-11

➡ Lived as a Pharisee—v. 5 (see Gal. 1:13-14)

➡ Imprisoned many saints—v. 10

➡ Condoned the deaths of many saints—v. 10

➡ Persecuted Christians—v. 11

## CIRCUMSTANCES SURROUNDING PAUL'S CONVERSION—VV. 12-18

1. Where was he going? _____

2. What time was it? _____

3. What did he see? _____

4. Who was with him? _____

5. What did he hear? _____

*(Read 2 Cor. 5:17; Gal. 6:15)*

## CHANGES IN PAUL'S ATTITUDES AND ACTIONS AFTER HIS CONVERSION—VV. 19-23

What evidence of Paul's repentance and conversion can be found in the following verses:

6. Verse 19— _____

7. Verse 20— _____

8. Verse 21— _____

9. Verses 22, 23— _____

*(Read 1 John 1:5-9; 2:3-6)*

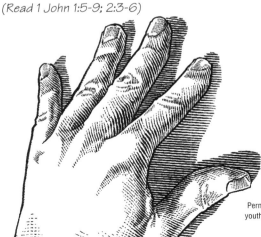

*Now go to the next page...*

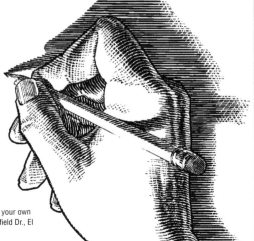

# Your Turn!

## INTRODUCTION

➡ Name

➡ Year in school (or age)

➡ School

➡ City

## ATTITUDES AND ACTIONS BEFORE I BECAME A CHRISTIAN—If appropriate, include family or church background. Avoid naming religious denominations, since this may alienate some of your listeners.

1.

2.

3.

4.

5.

## CIRCUMSTANCES SURROUNDING MY CONVERSION—Consider time, date, place, people, motivation, etc. This is a natural place to summarize the gospel: the death, burial, and resurrection of Jesus Christ.

1.

2.

3.

4.

5.

## CHANGES IN MY ATTITUDES AND ACTIONS SINCE MY CONVERSION—Be enthusiastic!

1.

2.

3.

4.

5.

## MISCELLANEOUS COMMENTS

# CHAPTER THREE

# YOUTH GROUP LEADERSHIP

## Appreciation File

Get extra encouragement out of those seldom-received notes of appreciation by putting them in a personal file. Over the months and years the file grows, and on days when you feel that no one appreciates your efforts, you can flip through this file and see and remind yourself of what your young people, parents, and coworkers really think of you. *Tim Lighthall, Chapin, S.C.*

## Bible Letters

Reading and meditating on the Bible is difficult for most teenage Christians—but what if they received Scripture in the form of a personal letter? Photocopy portions of Scripture that are directed to groups or individuals

(actualy, practically the whole New Testament fits this description). Then send that portion of scripture to the members of your youth group with a hand-written greeting and personal concluding note and signature. If they receive it as mail, they'll read it.

*Michael S. Hoskins, Grand Rapids, Mich.*

Dear Sarah,

If you have any encouragement from being united with Christ, if any comfort from his love, if any fellowship with the Spirit, if any tenderness and compassion, then make my joy complete by being like-minded, having the same love, being one in spirit and purpose. Do nothing out of selfish ambition or vain conceit, but in humility consider others better than yourselves. Each of you should look only to your own interests, but also to the interests of others.

Your youth leader,
Sandra

# Campus Visits

One way to make campus visits less intimidating is to distribute pictures of your students from recent youth events. Have double prints made of photos taken at various activities and take one set with you to the school. When you see students who attended these events, give them pictures that feature them. They'll love it. Their friends will want to see the pictures, too, and will ask all about the events. Kids will look forward to seeing you—or at least your pictures. *John Wood, Spring Lake, Mich.*

---

# Counseling Tapes

Have good advice readily available for your youths when they face difficult situations. Make cassette tapes of you, your pastor, a professional Christian counselor or physician in your church or community, or another youth leader (or perhaps several persons) discussing a particular issue and what a young person might do if faced with such a situation. Just the sound of a familiar voice may help a teen think clearly and avoid making rash decisions.

Possible topics include:

➤ *What do I do if I'm pregnant?*
➤ *I don't want to live anymore.*
➤ *I may have a sexually transmitted disease.*
➤ *What do I do when nobody likes me?*
➤ *How far is too far on a date?*
➤ *Why should I wait until marriage to have sex?*
➤ *I don't like the way I look.*
➤ *I've been sexually abused.*
➤ *My parents are getting a divorce.*
➤ *I'm not doing well in school.*
➤ *I'm expected to follow in my older brother's/sister's footsteps.*
➤ *My parents don't believe me.*
➤ *My girlfriend/boyfriend wants to break up with me.*
➤ *Does God really care about me?*
➤ *What's wrong with alcohol/drugs/tobacco?*
➤ *I might have an eating disorder*
➤ *I can't get along with my parents.*
➤ *I can't handle the peer pressure.*

Record the initial counsel you might give to a teen who comes to you about the particular issue the tape deals with. Include some biblical counsel as well as basic facts on the subject. Include a recorded conversation with a teen or young adult who has recently been through a similar situation and is willing to talk about it.

Encourage the teen to talk to you (or to whomever makes the recording) or to someone they trust who will give them good counsel. Don't use any names, of course, or direct your counsel at any one individual. These tapes are for a general audience.

Keep the tapes short—no more than 15 minutes. Listening to a tape may help the teen *want* to talk to you or someone else. Make copies of the tapes (one subject or situation per tape) available wherever youths gather.

To increase confidentiality, print the title of the subject or situation for each tape on a sheet of paper, assign a number to it, and display the list with the tapes. Then place the corresponding number on each tape so that a tape can be borrowed without anyone else seeing what problem or situation the person is dealing with. Encourage kids to give the appropriate tapes to any friends they know who are struggling with a certain issue. *Greg Miller, Knoxville, Tenn.*

---

# Gift Card

Reinforce a lesson on spiritual gifts and how God values us as individuals with this easy present. Gift-wrap a piece of cardboard and attach this poem or one of your own, with your name signed at the end. These will remind kids of their potential in God. *Pat McGlone, Savannah, Ga.*

*You have a gift all of your own;*
*Sometimes it's hard to see.*
*It's hidden deep inside of you,*
*But God can set it free.*

*Some days, of course, you wish that God*
*Would tell you what he knew*
*About your so-called specialness—*
*Why won't it show on cue?*

*Keep this package always wrapped*
*(There's nothing much within).*
*It's a reminder that you're the*
*Ideal gift to Him.*

# Seminar Trip

Centering youth ministry team retreats around area training seminars equips volunteers while building team unity. Identify the dates and locations of interesting seminars, then decide which city you want to visit—try a different city each year. Get as many of your team as possible to commit to a Friday through Sunday weekend, then reserve rooms at a nice hotel.

On Friday, enjoy a unique site in the city together, or try an ethnic restaurant. On Saturday attend the seminar—then treat the entire team to a superb dinner as a thank you for their service. Visit an energizing church on Sunday for worship and to explore how others do things. Then head for home.

Relaxing in the hotel rooms and in the church van allows for discussion of the seminar material and anything else you want to communicate to your team. Fund the event through your youth budget, by doing a fund-raiser, or by having the volunteers contribute toward the trip. *John Wood, Spring Lake, Mich.*

# CHAPTER FOUR

# SPECIAL EVENTS

## At the Sound of the Beep, Get Your Next Clue

Use the answering machine to add a new twist to a mystery journey.

Prepare five or so riddles that lead to pay phones at well-known locations around town. For example, the clue to Courtesy House/76 Truck Stop could be

*A big stop for your hungry truck or car*
*76 gas and a great salad bar.*
*Courtesy at this house means cleaning your plate,*
*And there are lots of gas pumps so you won't have to wait.*

Then enlist people in your church to record the clues on their answering machine. Players access these clues by phoning from mystery locations to get the next clue and phone number. First team to reach the final destination wins.

Prepare a Journeyman's Packet of clues and phone numbers, event rules, and a diagram of the other teams' routes in case of an emergency. Designate an adult Journey Master who stays at the church with the same packet the drivers have in case of confusion or emergency.

Divide your group into teams, then give the driver for each team a Journeyman's Packet.

**1.** The teams receive the first clue at the starting point and must direct their drivers to the location they surmise from the clue.

**2.** Upon arriving at the correct pay phone, the driver pulls from the Journeyman's Packet the phone number to call; one of the team members calls to hear the recorded clue to the next stop. As proof that a team is actually calling from a correct location, callers must tell the number of the pay phone they're calling

from—and leave a silly message, just for fun.

Other details:
➤ The locations can be the same for each team, but in a different order.
➤ Give each team enough money for the number of phone calls required.
➤ Give participants a time limit.
➤ Lost or confused teams return to the church for help or call a designated emergency number. If all else fails, the driver may open up an emergency envelope marked "Driver Only," which gives the clue to the last location. This final destination might be the church or the home of one of the kids or youth workers.

*Paul Turner, Vero Beach, Fla.*

## Commando Church

During your next lock-in—or during a dark evening at the church—teach about spiritual warfare from Ephesians 6:10-18.

As the kids get bored with your traditional message, tell them it's time to jump into battle. Explain the rules of war before proceeding to the sanctuary, where it's pitch black and you're broadcasting taped sound effects of war. Set up a "guard tower" between or on top of the pews in a central location. "Jail" is in an adjacent room. Assign several students to be guards. The head guard stands in the tower with a "searchlight" (flashlight).

The kids maneuver in, over, around, and under the pews and furnishings, trying to reach the "secret operative," to whom they give a password and receive a token (cut-up coffee stirrers work great). The secret operative could be right under the guard tower. Then

they make their way back to base, receive credit for the tokens, and go on another mission.

Meanwhile, the head guard watches for movement and shines the light on vulnerable players. Players hit by the light freeze and are escorted by other guards to the jail. After a designated time the guards can release the prisoners back into the game. The head guard may hold an "air raid," during which the flashlight is left off for 10 seconds to ensure that students can get through to the secret operative.

After the game you can draw many spiritual parallels, including that spiritual warfare is conducted in the sanctuary, among other places—by prayer, praise, etc. *Bruce Lininger, Albuquerque, N. Mex.*

# Cereal Scavenger Hunt

To get ready for this scavenger hunt, make a list of breakfast cereals and assign different point values to each. Break up the group into teams and give each team a list of the cereals, along with Baggies and pens. Then send the teams into a residential area to collect in their Baggies as many kinds of cereals as they can, marking off their lists as they go. They may not go to a store for any of the cereals, and they may get only one kind of cereal from each house.

Meet back at the church at a specific time. Provide bowls and spoons and milk and crunch away. Be sure to have a prize for the winning team. *Julie Suess, Visalia, Calif.*

# Dove Awards Party

Usually around April the Dove Awards (for Christian music) are broadcast. In 1994 the Family Channel ran a three-hour special. Invite your group members to meet at the church or at the home of someone with a big screen TV for a Dove Awards party.

As the kids arrive, hand each one a list of the nominees in different categories and ask them to guess who will win (photocopy the form on page 39). Keep a master list, and as you watch the televised ceremony, keep track of who guessed correctly. Give your own awards for the most correct guesses. Dove candy bars or Dove ice creams bars make a hit. *Brett C. Wilson, Terre Haute, Ind.*

# Feather Gladiators

At a lock-in or retreat in a large indoor room, divide the group into teams and ask all players to get their pillows. Allow teams to choose their names. Assign a scorekeeper to write the teams names on a chalkboard or marker board and keep score. Since this can get wild, have players remove their glasses before you begin.

Play the following games:
➤ **Use Your Head Relay.** Players take turns racing around a fixed object, such as a chair, at the opposite side of the room. During the first round, players balance a pillow on their head (no hands allowed).
➤ **Waddle Relay.** Runners hold the pillows between their knees (no hands allowed).
➤ **Cushy Caterpillar Slalom.** Each team races together, moving like a huge caterpillar with a pillow between each pair of players. They cannot touch the pillows with their hands, but must hold onto each other. Line up several chairs between the starting and ending points so that the caterpillars wind in and out. Do not make the caterpillars too long to avoid a domino effect if someone falls.
➤ **Goliath Clone War.** Have each team pick a Goliath. Have two Goliaths stand blindfolded on a low bench. With helpers standing by for safety, each tries to knock the other off the bench with his pillow.
➤ **Free-for-All Finale.** Limit this no-holds-barred pillow fight to three minutes.

*Kelvin Lustick, Kennett, Mo.*

# The
# Who-Will-Win-This-Year Dove Awards
# Guessing Form

## General awards:

Song of the year _____

Male vocalist of the year _____

Female vocalist of the year _____

Songwriter of the year _____

New artist of the year _____

Group of the year _____

Artist of the year _____

Producer of the year _____

## Song of the year—categories:

Rap _____

Metal _____

Rock _____

Contemporary _____

Inspirational _____

Southern Gospel _____

Country _____

Contemporary Black Gospel _____

Traditional Black Gospel _____

## Album of the year—categories:

Metal _____

Rock _____

Contemporary _____

Inspirational _____

Southern Gospel _____

Country _____

Contemporary Black Gospel _____

Traditional Black Gospel _____

## Video of the year:

Short form _____

Long form _____

# Movie Treasure Hunts

Use movie themes to give a wacky facelift to good ol' treasure hunts.

➤ For each game, create 10 or so clues and give copies to each team, but mix up the order so the teams aren't running into each other.

➤ At each location leave packets of clues color-coded for each team.

➤ Award each team 20 points for each clue uncovered.

➤ Inside each clue envelope include an emergency-clue envelope, which a team may open if necessary—but they'll forfeit 10 points if they open it. Use the following examples to get your creativity flowing.

## Back to the Future

All the clues in this hunt relate to the era or year of graduation of the clue holders—individuals in your church who will play along with your group's hunt. Tell teams this:

*Marty McFly is stuck in 1955. Your team must go back in time, find Marty, and return with him to the present—and to this location. The first team back with Marty wins.*

To the right are a couple clues to get your creative juices flowing.

## The Hunt for Fred October

Divide your group into Americans and Soviets—both teams are pursuing poor Fred.

Tell the Americans this:

*CIA operatives have found out that the Soviet Union has a new secret weapon: a submarine sandwich, which reports indicate is incredibly delectable. The KGB hopes to unleash the sub in America, the goal being that Americans will be so taken by this sandwich that they'll abandon McDonald's, Burger King, and Wendy's, thus causing the collapse of the American economy as we know it.*

*It is believed that Fred October, a Soviet spy planted deep in the U.S. fast-food industry, will bring over the prototype sub sandwich and introduce it into a Cleveland deli, from where news of it will spread like wildfire.*

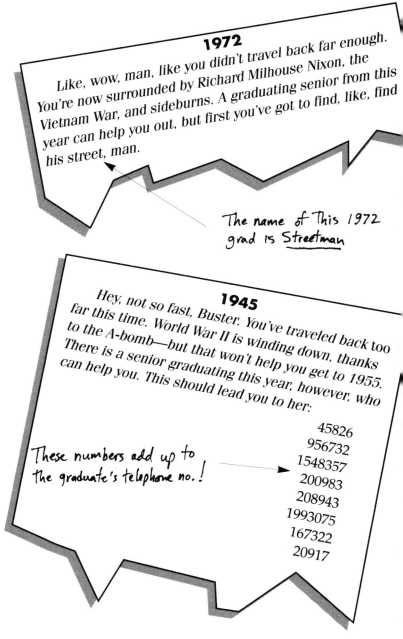

**1972**

Like, wow, man, like you didn't travel back far enough. You're now surrounded by Richard Milhouse Nixon, the Vietnam War, and sideburns. A graduating senior from this year can help you out, but first you've got to find, like, find his street, man.

*The name of this 1972 grad is Streetman*

**1945**

Hey, not so fast, Buster. You've traveled back too far this time. World War II is winding down, thanks to the A-bomb—but that won't help you get to 1955. There is a senior graduating this year, however, who can help you. This should lead you to her:

45826
956732
1548357
200983
208943
1993075
167322
20917

*These numbers add up to the graduate's telephone no.!*

*Your mission is to find Fred October, seize the submarine sandwich, and bring it safely back to headquarters.*

Tell the Soviets this:

*Comrades, our culinary experts are ready to unveil our ultimate secret weapon: a submarine sandwich. We are convinced that unsuspecting Western*

*capitalists will so love this sandwich that they will eat nothing else. As the decadent pigs become enslaved to this submarine sandwich, they will abandon McDonald's, Burger King, and Wendy's—thus precipitating the fall of Western capitalism and democracy itself.*

*Our plans to infiltrate the American fast-food industry with this sandwich have been temporarily halted because one of our own, Fred October, has defected to the U.S. with the prototype sub—the only one. Your mission, comrades, is to capture Fred October and return the sandwich to us.*

The teams follow typical treasure-hunt clues that lead them to the last house, where they find a submarine sandwich—a really horrible one, in fact, that you made just for the occasion: pickles, peanut butter, mayonnaise, a little dog food, raisins, etc. When the winners bring it back to headquarters, offer extra points to *whichever* team eats it.

## The Silence of the Yams

Police are trying to stop a huge jewel-smuggling operation. Their only clue is that the gem traffickers are smuggling diamonds in sweet potatoes. The police have recruited a supposedly reformed criminal to help in the search—Hannibal Lecter, who, unfortunately, has taken literally the slogan "Help take a bite out of crime."

The teams' mission is to catch the jewel smugglers—and before Hannibal Lecter has them for lunch.

The first team to return with the sweet potato containing the missing diamond wins.

Teams follow clues from location to location; clues are taped to the dismembered body parts of a mannequin. The final location has a sweet potato with a dime-store ring inside.

## Raiders of the Lost Bark

Send out teams to find a "lost" dog. Clues lead to a house, wherein is the dog—if you can arrange it, a large, smelly, friendly canine that they must transport back to home base. The smaller the cars and the more kids in them, the more fun the return trip is.

## Monastic Park

A millionaire obsessed with Francis of Assisi creates a sanctuary for gentle animals. He creates the gentle animals, too, by importing experts in hypertech cloning, who soon fill the park with gentle lions, gentle scorpions, gentle Tasmanian devils, gentle pit vipers, gentle pit bulls. However, when the brains behind the venture disappears (a kidnapping is suspected), the system begins reverting—moles become man-eaters, deer turn carnivorous and stalk humans. (And you thought the killer rabbit in *Search for the Holy Grail* was vicious.)

Teams must find the chief techie, led on by clues dealing with the myriad of animal-named products that surround us—cars (Cougar, Pinto, Rabbit, etc.), food and candy (Gummy bears, animal crackers,

Eagle Snacks), people (Mother Goose, River Phoenix) and other products (Turtle Wax). Clues lead teams to homes of people who own the appropriate cars, who have in their cupboards the appropriate food or product, who own books or videos of the appropriate people. The clues are hidden, of course, in or near the objects—and lead ultimately to the techie, who is biding his time in captivity playing video games.

### The Stinkstones

A Neolithic skunk family that lives in Fred and Wilma's attic tire of his bombast and decide to get even: they steal his bowling ball. Teams must get it back, with the help of powerfully odorific clues. The clues can be either *about* strong-smelling substances, or can reek themselves—of cheap perfume, ammonia, fertilizer, cod liver oil, etc.

*Lynn H. Pryor, San Antonio, Tex.*

# Theater in the Round in Reverse

This is dinner theater with a dramatic difference. Serve a delicious meal with tables set up in the middle of the room, leaving plenty of space on all sides of the room. Then surround the diners with drama. Use several areas of the room, making the kids wonder where the actors will come from next. *John Peters, Cleveland, Tenn.*

# Holy Lift Tickets

Ski trips are notorious for being fun but spiritually unproductive times for many youth groups. In order to get enough runs for the cost of the lift ticket, skiers usually go from the opening of the lift to closing time with barely a stop for food, much less for a quiet time or Bible study.

To help students reflect on God's creation, hand out daily "Holy Lift Tickets." Photocopy page 43 for one day's reflection plus "blanks" into which you can insert your own verses and reflections for the other days of your trip. It's not only a fun activity for kids, but also a meaningful one. *Eugene C. Scott, Tulsa, Okla.*

# HOLY LIFT TICKET

This ticket entitles bearer to time with God.
Good only on _____

"A cheerful heart is good medicine, but a crushed spirit dries up the bones." (Proverbs 17:22)
_____

**F**or at least today, don't picture God as some cosmic cop, eager to lock us up or knock us over the head whenever we stray dangerously close to having fun. Look around you...God's creation is amazing. He must have enjoyed himself immensely when he invented mountains and snow. The stroke of genius, though, was creating in us the ability to enjoy his mountains and snow.

So take advantage of God's creation today. Ski, laugh, hang out with your friends. And sometime—maybe even right now—say a simple prayer of thanks for all the good things God has given you.

# HOLY LIFT TICKET

This ticket entitles bearer to time with God.
Good only on _____
_____

# HOLY LIFT TICKET

This ticket entitles bearer to time with God.
Good only on _____
_____

# CHAPTER FIVE

# HOLIDAYS

# HALLOWEEN

## *Halloween Hospital Visits*

Instead of a Halloween spookout next year, turn things around and have your youths hand out treats instead of receive them. At the beginning of October contact your local hospital to see if it will allow your group to visit the pediatric unit on Halloween, and find out what time is best for your visit.

Once your trip is confirmed, contact a local restaurant or store to get some trick-or-treat bags (many are happy to provide them at no cost). Then have your kids start collecting items to fill trick-or-treat bags: coloring books, crayons, stickers, games, and helium balloons work well. Be sure to check with nurses before putting candy into a child's bag. Include in each bag a note on your youth group's letterhead explaining who you are and the reason for your visit and gifts.

A few days before your visit, call the hospital to confirm how many children are in the ward and how old they are. This will ensure that you make up

enough bags and that they are age appropriate.

On the day of your visit have everyone come dressed up in costumes. Let the kids know that they should not wear scary costumes or medical garb.

After you hand out the bags and talk for a while with the children, surprise your students with a special party at someone's home or a nearby restaurant.

*Jennifer Carpenter and Tommy Baker, Florence, Ky.*

---

## *Pumpkin Olympics*

Hold a Pumpkin Olympics the week after Halloween, when supermarkets and nurseries are practically giving away leftover pumpkins. Plan on three pumpkins for each person.

Divide into at least four teams. Since these games are messy, hold the Olympics outdoors. Here are events to use.

➤ **Dodge Pumpkin**. Everyone sits in a large circle, with one person in the middle. Choose a large pumpkin and roll it at the person in the middle, trying to hit

the person. Increase the number of pumpkins for interest. If a pumpkin splats, replace it.

➤ **Pumpkin Bowling.** Set up empty two-liter bottles, cans, or bowling pins. Each person rolls a pumpkin once and tallies the total number of pins knocked down. A leader can be constantly resetting the pins.

➤ **Pumpkin Toss.** Similar to an egg toss, two people from a team toss a pumpkin back and forth, stepping further apart each time, until someone drops it.

➤ **Pumpkin Put.** Put (as in *putting* the shot) a pumpkin through the air and measure how far it goes. Competition may be based on using the largest person from each team, the smallest person, the largest pumpkin, or the smallest pumpkin.

➤ **Pumpkin Catapult.** Rest a sturdy board on a cinder block, teeter-totter fashion. Place a pumpkin on the board's lower end, step down hard (or jump) on the raised end, and measure how far the pumpkin flies.

➤ **The Great Pumpkin Relay.** Set up an obstacle course. Players carry a large pumpkin as they negotiate the course, then they hand the pumpkin to the next player.

➤ **Pumpkin Soccer.** Dribble the pumpkin around a cone or other marker and back to the starting point, where the next person takes a turn.

➤ **Potentially Popular Pumpkin Pick-up Contest.** By the end of the Olympics, the grounds are a mess, so have a clean-up contest. Provide plastic trash bags and award megapoints to the team that collects the most pumpkin debris. Have a scale on hand to weigh the bags if possible.

After the Olympics, award the World's Largest Banana Split to the winning team. This will be much more appealing than a piece of pumpkin pie. *Allen L. Pickett, Allison Park, Pa.*

# CHRISTMAS

## Candy Cane Lane

Choose a neighborhood in your area that is known for extravagant Christmas decorations. Take your group on a tour of the area, giving each person a judging sheet. Have judging categories for "Most Creative," "Simple Beauty," "Best Use of a Theme," etc.

Meet back at church or a designated home for hot chocolate and Christmas goodies. Collect the judging sheets, tally the results and announce the winners.

You may want to return to the area to award the winners a small prize from your youth group (and invite them to your church!). *Theo Olson, San Jose, Calif.*

## Handmade Christmas Wrap

This fund-raiser costs you pennies and gives your kids a chance to use their artistic abilities. Purchase a bolt of brown wrapping paper from a wholesaler, butcher, or newspaper publisher. Cut simple Christmas shapes from clean kitchen sponges (Christmas trees, holly, stars, bells, and wreaths work well). Have students use the sponge shapes dipped in acrylic paints to create unique repeated designs. Be sure to let each color dry before adding additional colors. Measure the paper and cut it into two-yard lengths. Roll it into tubes and tie it with natural jute.

Publicize your sale in your church newsletters and bulletins. Sell your original wrapping paper in November and December. For display purposes wrap boxes of various sizes, tie them with jute, and place them with the rolls of Christmas wrap on your selling table. *Heather Monkmeyer, Farmington, Mich.*

## Christmas Word Search

On page 46 is a word search—an activity that can actually calm down the kids—with a Christmas theme. *Cary W. Sharpe, Severn, Md.*

# Christmas Word Search

*Instructions: Words may be spelled forwards or backwards, vertically or horizontally or diagonally. A letter may belong to more than one word.*

```
Z X W S Y P G N I K C O T S A R I
G Y A D H T R I B Y P P A H P Q H
C V N F T D A W F S P M N S Y O T
H A G H Q E O B J T T A G T U R A
C J E S U S D W I S E M E N B C E
E D I H A B K B I A O J L E G O R
O R J E S T A R V N L L I S N O W
T K Q P E C H Y K T M I H E H R S
E X S H A C D F M A N G E R B N Z
L L A E Y W T L H U A H J P F A P
T G M R E I N D E E R T X N C M T
S S R D B S D F V Y Q S E V L E C
I E C S L O R A C F O A P M O N Z
M E N F W H O L I D A Y H R K T U
```

ANGEL
BOW
CANDY
CAROLS
ELVES
GIFT
HAPPY BIRTHDAY

HOLIDAY
JESUS
KING
LIGHTS
MANGER
MERRY CHRISTMAS
MISTLETOE
ORNAMENT
PRESENTS
REINDEER

SANTA
SHEPHERDS
SNOW
STAR
STOCKING
TOYS
TREE
WISEMEN
WREATH

# Christmas Carol Trivia

How well do the teens in your group know the details in Christmas carols? Divide your group into two teams, and award a point for each correct answer to the trivia questions below. If one team misses, the other can the steal the point with a correct answer. Set a time limit—10 to 20 seconds is probably enough.

After the game, *sing* them—the kids have probably hummed through them already trying to come up with the answers. *Greg Thompson, Macon, Ga.*

## Christmas Carol Trivia

1. In the carol, "The Twelve Days of Christmas," what happens on the eighth day? *(eight maids-a-milking)*

2. In "Jingle Bells," where are the bells? *(bells on bobtail ring)*

3. When we "Deck the Halls," who is to hail the new? *(ye lads and lasses)*

4. What happens on the eleventh day of Christmas? *(11 pipers piping)*

5. When the Lord comes in "Joy to the World," who repeats the sounding joy? *(fields and floods, rocks, hills, and plains)*

6. At what time of the day was Jesus born, according to "O Come, All Ye Faithful"? *(this happy morning)*

7. What kind of sleep did the people of "O Little Town of Bethlehem" experience? *(deep and dreamless)*

8. According to "Away in a Manger," who is lowing? *(cattle)*

9. Who is blessed in the third verse of "Away in a Manger"? *(all the dear children)*

10. Who kept time for the "Little Drummer Boy"? *(the ox and lamb)*

11. What are we going to tell on the mountain? *(that Jesus Christ is born)*

12. Name three songs with the word "Christmas" in the title. *("The Twelve Days of Christmas," "Have Yourself a Merry Little Christmas," "Christmas Is the Best Time of the Year," "The Christmas Song," "We Wish You a Merry Christmas," etc.)*

13. Name two songs with the word "bell" in the title. *("Jingle Bells," "Silver Bells," "I Heard the Bells on Christmas Day," etc.)*

14. How many times do you "fa la la la la" in one verse of "Deck the Halls"? *(four)*

15. In the song "Up on the Housetop," who came down the chimney? *(good St. Nick)*

16. What sound does the drum make in "Little Drummer Boy"? *(pa rum pa pum pum)*

17. What is the last line in the first verse of "Silent Night"? *(sleep in heavenly peace)*

18. Why should you watch out, not cry, and not pout? *(Santa Claus is coming to town)*

19. What was the weather like one Christmas Eve when Santa asked Rudolph to guide his sleigh? *(foggy)*

20. Who said the "First Noel"? *(the angel)*

21. Silver bells, silver bells, it's Christmas time in the _____. *(city)*

22. "I'm Dreaming of a _____ Christmas." *(white)*

23. All I want for Christmas is _____. *(my two front teeth)*

24. How many ships were seen on Christmas morn? *(three)*

25. In "Have Yourself a Merry Little Christmas," what is "out of sight"? *(your troubles)*

# Christmas Stockings

Spare the Christmas party host home's floor some of

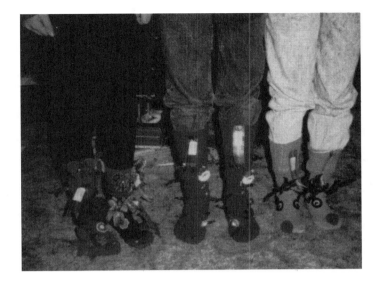

the dirt and mud of the season by asking the teens to decorate and wear their own Christmas stockings. Award prizes for categories such as brightest, most colorful, most original, etc. Who knows? Battery-operated Christmas light footwear may be the hottest new fad. *Carolyn Peters, Beaver Dam, Wis.*

# Jesus Birthday Presents

Copy page 49 and give to your students in order to make Matthew 25:40 come alive for them. Here are concrete specifics for giving Christ a Christmas present by serving "the least." *Tom Lytle, Marion, Ohio*

# M & M Game

With only a few bags of M&Ms (reds and greens only, if available), a spoon for each team, and paper cups, put on a holiday relay.

Put one pound of M&Ms for each six teens in one large bowl. Divide into teams of three to eight and line the teams up single file, seated on the floor. The first person in line should be about five feet away from the bowl of M&Ms. The object is for each team to get the most green M&Ms from the bowl.

The first person in line uses a spoon to scoop up one green M&M, runs back to the team line, and

dumps the M&M in a paper cup. He then sits down where he started and hands the spoon to the second person in line. This continues until time is called.

To add interest, a leader may occasionally change the number of M&Ms to collect, calling out "Three!" or a another number, and after a few minutes may yell, "Back to one!"

The players will be tempted to interfere with each other's spoons, scoop up more than one M&M, or cheat in other ways. You can be strict about the rules, or you can allow some fudging, then lead into a lesson on cheating and how easily we become caught up in it.

Afterwards, feast on M&Ms of any and all colors. *Chard Berndt, Twin Falls, Ida.*

# Twelve Days of Youth Group

Here's a way to relive the youth group's memorable moments of the past year—have the adult sponsors make up verses to the tune of "The Twelve Days of Christmas."

Begin each verse with "On the ____ day of Christmas, the youth group gave to me..." Here are some examples.

➤ **First Day** —"Another pizza party." (Sponsor holds an old pizza box with leftover pizza in it.)

➤ **Second Day**—"Junior high romances." (Sponsor unrolls toilet paper with a girl's name on it and the crossed off names of several boys; while singing, the sponsor cries and wipes tears with the toilet paper.)

➤ **Third Day**—"Another all night lock-in." (Sponsor holds basketball, No-Doz, and videos.)

➤ **Fourth Day**—"Head banger music." (Sponsor wears long-haired wig and a Walkman and "bangs" his head while singing.)

➤ **Fifth Day**—"A losing softball team." (Sponsor wears jersey and cap and breaks a plastic bat over his knee.)
*Tom Lytle, Marion, Ohio*

# The Copyman Christmas

On page 50 begins a sketch for nine actors about gift giving, highlighted by the "Saturday Night Live" character Copyman. *Joel and Kara M. Hunt, Omaha, Neb.*

# Give Jesus a Birthday Present

That's right—this year you'll hear all about the gifts he gave us (himself, his mercy, his son), but why not give him a present, too? "I tell you the truth," Jesus told his followers, "whatever you did for one of the least of these brothers of mine, you did for me" (Matt. 25:40). So here are 12 practical ideas for the 12 days of Christmas!

❄ Give the money you earn during one day or shift to the Salvation Army.

❄ Volunteer one day or night per month (or per week) for a year at a nursing home or hospital.

❄ Volunteer time and service at our church (wash dishes in the kitchen, clean the van or bus, etc.)

❄ Organize a small-scale clothing drive with some friends, and donate your earnings to the charity of your choice.

❄ Baby-sit free for an evening for a single mother once a month for a year.

❄ Shovel an elderly person's walk next time it snows.

❄ Visit a shut-in just to chit-chat and play a game.

❄ Prepare a meal for a shut-in.

❄ Run errands or clean house for an elderly person.

❄ Make a "Kind Deeds Coupon Book" and give it to your parents ("This coupon good for one clean room whenever asked," " …good for one free night of baby-sitting without complaining," or " …good for one week's worth of trash duty").

❄ Write a monthly letter to the relative who would appreciate it the most.

❄ Volunteer to teach in next summer's vacation Bible school.

"Whatever you did for one of the least of these brothers of mine, you did for me."

To:

From:

To:

From

# The Copyman Christmas

CHARACTERS
Copyman      Mr. Smith      Junior
Paycheck Guy (Rob)      Mary Jane      Dillon
Gossip Woman (Ginger)      James      Joe

*As the scene begins, **all the characters** are on stage, at a Christmas party.*

**COPYMAN:** *(in a voice like "Saturday Night Live's" Copyman)* Twelve o'clock! It's time for the annual office Christmas party. Hey, Mr. Smith bought presents for all the employees. What a guy!

**MR. SMITH:** Gather around, people. Due to increased sales, our accountant has allowed me to buy Christmas gifts for each one of you this year.

**PAYCHECK GUY:** Oh, boy. I'll bet we get a fruitcake again this year.

**GOSSIP WOMAN:** No, I heard we're getting more than fruitcake this year. We might even be getting a cash bonus.

**COPYMAN:** *(sarcastically)* Dream on.

**MR. SMITH:** Here we go. I'll be handing these out in no particular order. Let's see now...Here you go, Mary Jane. Merry Christmas.

**COPYMAN:** Gee, a smokeless ashtray. A gift for all of us. Thank you.

**MR. SMITH:** And for James...Merry Christmas.

**JAMES:** Chapstick?

**COPYMAN:** Chapstick, for kissing up to the boss.

**MR. SMITH:** Merry Christmas, Dillon.

**DILLON:** Concentrated breath spray?

**COPYMAN:** Yes, a subliminal message for the Romeo...

**MR. SMITH:** And for you, Ginger.

**GINGER:** Oh, Mr. Smith! Perfume! *(sprays some on her neck)* Here, smell my neck.

**COPYMAN:** Wow! Silent but deadly.

**MR. SMITH:** That smells really nice, Ginger.

**COPYMAN:** Bossman needs a cold shower.

**PAYCHECK GUY:** Come on. Come on. Let's get the show on the road.

**MR. SMITH:** Of course, of course. Well, let's see. Next we have a gift for Rob.

**PAYCHECK GUY:** Great. A coffee mug. Thanks, Mr. Smith. Gotta go.

**COPYMAN:** Robbie, the Paycheck Guy, only comes to collect.

**JUNIOR:** How about me, Dad? I mean, Boss?

**MR. SMITH:** Yes, Junior. Here's a special gift for all of your hard work and extra long hours at the office.

**JUNIOR:** Wow! A promotion with the new title of Professional Executive Assistant Engineer. Thanks, Dad.

**JAMES:** Now wait just a doggone minute, sir. I've done twice the work he has.

**GOSSIP WOMAN:** Yeah, he's stolen more of my ideas.

**COPYMAN:** The Bossmeister's son...making a ruckus.

(*Chaos breaks out in the office. Mr. Smith throws up his hands in despair and exits, with Junior on his heels and Ginger following.*)

**JOE:** Hey, everybody! This is no way to behave. It's Christmas.

**COPYMAN:** Joe Christian, always to the rescue.

**JOE:** Have you all forgotten the reason we celebrate Christmas?

**JAMES:** Why we celebrate Christmas? Well, it's a holiday, that's why. It's in red letters on my calendar. We just *have* to celebrate it.

**JOE:** But you've forgotten how Christmas started. It's a birthday.

**DILLON:** I learned that in Sunday school. It's Jesus' birthday.

**JOE:** Right. God sent his only Son, Jesus, to the world almost 2,000 years ago.

**DILLON:** And when it was time for Jesus to be born, Mary and Joseph couldn't find a room in the inn.

**COPYMAN:** No vacancy in the Holiday Inn.

**JOE:** So Mary had her baby in the stable. She named him Jesus and laid him in a manger.

**COPYMAN:** Baby Jesus...sleepin' in the manger scene.

**MARY JANE:** I remember what happened next! Angels appeared to shepherds out in the fields and told them about Jesus. They ran into town to find the baby in the manger.

**COPYMAN:** Manger scene...Nativirama.

**JAMES:** Oh, yes, it's all coming back to me! These wise men from the East saw a bright star in the sky and followed it to find the baby.

**DILLON:** These guys gave Jesus gifts—gold, frankincense, and myrrh.

**COPYMAN:** Wise masters...went Christmas shopping for Baby Jesus.

**JOE:** They understood who the baby was—the Son of God. When he grew up, he promised abundant life and eternal life to everyone who accepted him, then he died on a cross to pay for sin and bring salvation to everyone who believed.

**JAMES:** Is that true? Can Jesus really give salvation to me? How about to someone as obnoxious as the Copyman?

**JOE:** Yes. The point is not how obnoxious or sinful a person is. Jesus came to bring new life to *everyone* who believes.

**MARY JANE:** If that's true, then Christmas is a lot more than presents and office parties. It's really about the birthday of Jesus, the Son of God.

**COPYMAN:** The true meaning of Christmas...Putting the Christ back in *Ex*-mas.

# CHAPTER SIX

# PUBLICITY

## Coded Messages

Need a new way to catch their attention? Find a computer program or font package that prints special symbols or other languages and send "coded" messages, postcards, etc., to your kids.

In such a program every letter on the keyboard corresponds to a character in the special font. Make sure to include on the card where the kids can come to decipher the message (usually to your group meeting). Don't forget to bring the decoder sheet when you meet! *Greg Miller, Knoxville, Tenn.*

SKI TRIP
SIGN UP BY THIS SUNDAY
AND PAY THE $25
DEPOSIT

*This...*

*becomes this...*

*...or this*

Want to read this special message?
Bring this card to the youth room on Sunday and decode it!

Want to read this special message?
Bring this card to the youth room on Sunday and decode it!

*code key*

A B C D E F G H I J K L M N O P

Q R S T U V W X Y Z 1 2 3 4 5 6 7 8 9 0 $

*code key*

A B C D E F G H I J K L M

N O P Q R S T U V W X Y Z

## Call In and Win!

Kids not reading their monthly activity calendar? Among the event listings for a given day in the month, add something like this:

**BE CALLER NUMBER 5 TODAY AND WIN A FREE PIZZA!**

—or a discount coupon to your local Family Fun Center, or a gift certificate to their favorite fast-food restaurant. Be sure to list what phone number to call—not the church secretary, but ideally an answering machine that reviews the month's events before giving callers the chance to log their messages. *Tom Greilich, Kerman, Calif.*

## Surprise Photos

Kids love seeing themselves in photos. Collect posters and cardboard displays from current movies or TV programs. Snap photos of your youth group members and tape their faces over the faces of the stars.

For example, a poster from "Beverly Hills, 90210" pictures seven kids in a beach scene. Substitute five faces from your youth group and leave two original faces on each end.

Announce youth group events and activities on the corners of the posters. *Valerie Hobbie, Grand Rapids, Mich.*

## Prophetic Advertising

Instead of the standard promotional material on your next event, create a "prophetic" news article about how it will happen. Include all information about the event in the news clipping. Write it up like a story in your local newspaper, using as many details as possible. To stir up some curiosity, add specific names and descriptions of what will (or could likely) occur. *Len Cuthbert, Hamilton, Ont., Canada*

*Elliott Youth Nuuz*
**FRIDAY JUNE 16, 1994**

# Youth Spend a Day At The Ranch

The Youth of Elliott were back at the (Rocky Ridge) ranch today to spend the day horseback riding. Some of the youth had little experience on a horse and for some, they had never been near a horse. But it didn't matter since the ranch has people with little or no experience come all the time. Normally the youth attend Sunday school at 9:45 am, but today, they were riding horses, then had a short chapel service and a great hot meal followed. After lunch, they were back on the horses again for

the afternoon. The chapel service was unique because it involved the Chapman family, who own and operate the ranch. They all take part in the service by leading or playing the music or whatever. It's a different kind of service because the participants of the service felt like part of the family. It was a great way to spend a day of winter vacation.

Sounds like an expensive day? It only cost them $17 ($5 was paid by May 30 and the remaining $12 was paid on the day of the event).

# The Big Picture

Create a floor-to-ceiling note pad using 4 x 8 foot sheets of white bathroom paneling. Dry eraser markers work well on these boards. It makes a great billboard for serious messages (prayer lists, announcements) or a canvas for creative doodlers. *Tim Stoica, Colorado Springs, Colo.*

# Frisbee Publicity

Here's a new way to get your summer activities calendar into the hands of your kids—so they don't lose it! You might find a local company to produce this

informational Frisbee, or you can contact Custom Ad Design, 77 Crestview Road, Columbus, OH 43202, (614) 263-7170. No camera-ready artwork is required.

*Jay Firebaugh, Blacklick, Ohio*

# Kodalith Moment

Personalize your youth room with wall art depicting your teens. Buy some Kodalith film (a negative slide-producing film), take silhouette photos of your students, and process the film into slides that can be projected onto your walls. Trace the silhouettes onto the walls, and then paint everything in your negative slide that is light. You'll be amazed at the finished product! *Dik LaPine, Auburn Hills, Mich.*

# CHAPTER SEVEN

# FUNDRAISERS

## Battle of the Sexes

Build a wooden balance that will hold two paint buckets. Let the girls in the youth group decorate their bucket and the guys decorate theirs. Cut coin slots in the lids and encourage people in the congregation to drop pocket change into the bucket of their choice. After a predetermined number of Sundays has passed, declare either the heaviest bucket or the one with the most money the winner. If the guys win, the girls wear baseball hats and serve donuts and coffee after church the next week. If the girls win, the guys don aprons and serve sweet rolls and coffee. Adult men and women donate the goodies, and ultimately everyone wins. *Kimberlee Ingraham, Nevada City, Calif.*

## Business Card Place Mats

Here's a twist on the pancake breakfast idea that really makes some money. Make up a master place mat for use at the breakfast. On the mat, draw space for a business card. Have youth group members take copies of the master along with a letter of explanation to local businesses and sell the space for advertising. Charge $50 or whatever businesses in your community will support. The space can be filled with the business's card, a small display ad, or something you provide. Several master place mats can be designed, each featuring a different advertiser. Or you can charge each advertiser less and place several advertisements on each place mat. By making copies of the masters, you will have place mats for several church events. *Jeff Keas, Jackson, Tenn.*

## Game Leaders for Hire

Train your youth group to stage and execute adventure games for other groups and events to raise money. *David Boshart, Spokane, Wash.*

# Pray for Our Teenagers

The idea here is to enlist five households among your congregation to regularly pray for each teenager in your church—as well as get to know "their" teenager personally and remember special events in the teenagers' life (birthdays, plays and performances, games, graduation, etc.).

Send a letter to parents of teenagers in your church, explaining the idea and asking them to fill out an accompanying form (you can photocopy the one on page 57 if you want; you or the organizing youth staff member should sign it). Transfer each form's information to a convenient-sized card, then distribute copies of that card to five households in the congregation. Update each teenager's card every six months. *Andrew Pifer, Clinton, Mass.*

# Youth Prayer Calendar

Get others to pray for the specific needs of your youth group by handing out a prayer calendar to all your adult sponsors, to the prayer warriors of the church, and to your leadership youths.

Divide your list of students into five equal groups, and list them as illustrated below. Make copies and hand them out. If you have a large group, consider splitting your youth list onto several different calendars and give the calendars out to different people.

If you have a calendar program on your computer, create your own individualized church calendar. It also allows you to add names to your list as your group grows. *Randy Young, Hutchinson, Kans.*

# Y.E.S.

Link up teens with adults by launching a Youth Encouragement Sponsor (Y.E.S.) program. Adults commit to pray for students at least once a week, to contact them at least once a month, and to send a birthday card. This program could be introduced after a sermon on the impact of prayer, or anytime at all. *Bruce Lininger, Albuquerque, N. Mex.*

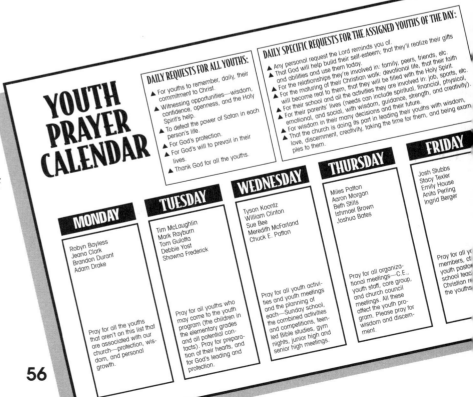

Dear Parents,

　　We want to enlist five households among our congregation to regularly pray for your teenager—as well as get to know your child personally and remember special events in the his or her life (birthdays, plays and performances, games, graduation, etc.).

　　To do this, we need some information from you. Will you complete the form below and return it to us?

　　Thanks! We want to update your teenager's five "pray-ers" every six months, so you can expect a similar form that often.

Return this form to _____

No later than: _____

Sincerely,

Name _____

Birthday _____ Age _____

Address _____

_____

Phone _____

Interests, activities, clubs, hobbies, etc. _____

Parent(s) _____

Address of parent(s) (if different from teenager's) _____

_____

Prayer requests _____

_____

_____